THE TRINITY AT HOME

Duncan Basil

The
Trinity at Home

A Family Likeness

ST PAULS

ST PAULS Publishing
Morpeth Terrace, London SW1P 1EP, U.K.

Copyright © ST PAULS U.K. 1999

ISBN 085439 561 X

Set by TuKan, High Wycombe
Produced in the EC
Printed by Watkiss Studios Ltd., Bedfordshire. U.K.

ST PAULS is an activity of the priests and brothers
of the Society of St Paul who proclaim the Gospel
through the media of social communication

To
Sister Mary Cecily Boulding O.P.

Contents

Contents

Preface

Saint Augustine, wandering along the seashore and pondering the Blessed Trinity, met a small boy scooping up sea water with a shell and pouring it into a small hole in the sand. "Yes", said the angel for such he was – "you will sooner empty the sea like this before fathoming the depths of that mystery."

Forgive then this impudent effort to paddle in the same ocean of divine love. Brothers, sisters and friends have done their kindliest best to be sure there are no errors or falsifications but every comparison limps and nothing can conceal the inadequacy of this attempt.

May it nevertheless help to draw us closer to this home and hearth of incredible love.

Image of Three

"A large white blob is the only way I can imagine the Holy Spirit," remarked a worried parishioner whilst a staunch feminist exploded with this. "To me the mystery of the Blessed Trinity evokes the most boring, male chauvinistic club in the world." Clearly it is time to broaden our outlook. God is love and if the life of his Incarnate Son is anything to go by then surely there must be a warmth and fascination about this mystery drawing us into wonder and communion.

Popular devotion has made do with St Patrick's three-leafed clover which is indeed a powerful symbol of unity in multiplicity but it scarcely seems to exhaust the mystery Christ came to reveal. Still less does it evoke loyalty and devotion any more than that other popular symbol – the equilateral triangle. With its three equal sides in one basic figure it does say something about the mystery but it is not an attractive figure. Theology comes to the rescue but can scare us with technical terms as it discusses the 'economic' or the 'immanent' Trinity. As if to close the subject it warns us of this fatal trap that has snapped up many a heretic.

Perhaps Christ is so central to our spiritual lives that we forget his Trinitarian concern to bring us home to the Father through the gift and guidance of the Holy Spirit. But the Church has always insisted that God is three in one: Father, Son and Holy Spirit, and yet we fight shy of a mystery that seems to have little to do with humdrum human life. At a deeper level it comes across as a theological mine-field where angels alone may safely tread. Having said the *Our Father* and a few *Glory be's* most of us are happy to leave it at that.

And yet a mediaeval saint reckoned that you could find hints of the Trinity anywhere and every-where and his logic was very simple. If creation was made out of nothing then God had no blueprint or plan to copy other than himself. Since he is three persons in one divine nature then his likeness in unity and pluralism is beckoning to us at every twist and turn of life. It is a bit like the three-dimensional picture of a hologram printed on a glass plate. If you drop it then every fragment of glass will bear the complete image of the original. Drop a jigsaw puzzle and spend hours of effort to regain the chocolate box picture. Drop the holo-gram and it stares at you instantly from a thousand splinters. So too the fragments of creation around us are crying out their divine and Trinitarian origins.

Blackpool rock tells a similar story. Wherever you break it, the letters proclaim throughout, "A present from Blackpool". Just so the Trinitarian seal is stamped into all creation. "Speak to me of God," I said, "and the almond tree blossomed."

It was these hints of the Trinity that long ago crowded into my daily life to such an extent that I began to grow suspicious of this work-a-day world around me. It seemed to be hiding something and yet winking as if there was much more to things than their surface appearance. As I struggled through a course in English literature this suspicion grew into conviction. Writers, poets and playwrights seemed to assume a mysterious other world, penetrating our own earthly realm and yet somehow native to it. Sacred and profane, human and divine, material and spiritual – all were talking the same language as if they were first cousins. Poetry would cheerfully describe human infatuations in terms of divine love. In the old song, for example:

"The thirst that from the soul doth rise,
doth ask a drink divine."

If, in this basic area of love, you could so easily interchange heaven's language for earth's then there just had to be a kind of double meaning about everything. Divinity belongs to the language of prayer and the thirst for it is almost a summary of the psalms, "My soul is thirsting for the Lord". Yet without batting an eyelid we seem to be able to switch from sacred words of prayer to the commonplaces of human love. It seems a kind of sacrilege to be evoking a drink divine in a lovers' banquet as if divinity were on a par with amorous humanity.

This paradox, as yet without Trinitarian overtones, kept on surfacing through many a donnish and dreary lecture. Sylvia's swains 'adored' her; according to Shakespeare, custom could not stale Cleopatra's 'infinite perfections' and lovers in general seemed to 'worship' the ground on which she trod. All this was not just a matter of spiritual words pressed into use for earthly situations because the whole dynamic of courtship and love seemed as applicable to the sacred as to the secular. A typical sonnet cycle would come up with all the classical attitudes and terms of spirituality. Hearts were smitten by the arrow of love, the 'rich golden shaft' that recalled the piercing of the heart of a St Teresa of Avila. You found the knightly lover with saintly humility scouring the pots in the scullery at the behest of an imperious lady-love. For all the world you might have been reading about Thérèse of Lisieux's famous spiritual battle in the laundry. Even martyrdom, that protestation of fidelity unto death, crops up as a kind of leitmotif in love poetry as in prayer. "And for bonnie Annie Laurie I would lay me doun and dee."

Looking at this ambiguity more critically you find scholars debating the origins of the Bible's "Song of Songs." Is it a human love song somehow elevated to sacred status or is it the most sublime expression of divine love ever written? "My beloved to me and I to my beloved". And "Let him kiss me with the kiss of his lips". Such language

14

either ignores the gulf between human and divine realities or it is trying to tell us of a hidden kinship between them.

The symbol of the human heart sums all this up in a very poignant fashion. You find hearts carved on trees in the parks, pierced by an arrow of love, just as you find them in the sacred pictures and images of our churches. Saints and sinners, we all use the heart as the focus of love – of God's love for us and of our love for him and for one another. "Long live the merry, merry heart that laughs by night and day" is almost an echo of the Scriptures', "God loves the cheerful giver".

It was, then, this casual use of similar language to express secular or profane that first roused my suspicions that there must be some mysterious similarity between man, this 'split radish', and his divine creator. A world of nature was winking at me but I needed to return to Eden, where Creator and creature first met, before I could suss out the reason why.

My atheist friend always jeered at the story of Adam and Eve in the garden and to back him up scholars have spilled rivers of ink debunking those first chapters of the Bible. And something of their scepticism had rubbed off on me. Who, after all, could chronicle the events of prehistory and who in the chill wind of popular evolutionism could really believe the key passage claiming that we were made in the 'image and likeness' of God? But it was precisely those powerful words that forged for me the link between sacred and profane; "Let us make man in our image, after our likeness... so God created man in his own image, in the image of God he created him; male and female he created them". Despite all efforts to tame this haunting text it seemed to have the power of solving the paradox wherein we humans so casually use the language of heaven.

If we are in some mysterious way made in the 'image and likeness' of the Triune God then surely the human image can tell us a great deal about him. You can read or talk about something until the cows come home but nothing brings us so close to reality as an image. The scale model of Fountains Abbey says more at a glance than any guided tour. I began to feel the need to take very seriously this image and likeness, this blueprint of God that we are and it reminded me of the games we used to play at school.

2

Copy and Original

Alan was a classmate who spent much of his free time tinkering with model aircraft which was natural enough since he was the son of an RAF pilot. In those pre-war days, before space travel took over, planes were the great fascination for small boys. Very soon every kind of elastic-driven model began to appear – from crude contraptions to the then hush hush Spitfire.

Now we boys had never got close to a plane, to the real original thing and yet technical terms and a surprising knowledge of aerodynamics swiftly appeared. When the crunch of wartime flying came we took to it almost instinctively. Quite naturally we found that we could speak the same language as the flying instructor and could often anticipate his guidance. The schoolboy's model plane, the image and likeness, had generated an astonishing familiarity with the exemplar, the real thing – a Spitfire no less.

"Let us make man in our own image and likeness." These are the words of a master craftsman who could create, with exactitude, scaled down models even of his own infinite self. Little wonder then if the language and behaviour of human beings should resemble so closely the divine. Men and women, in a limited way, speak the language of their origins. We are copycats by design. Even before the fullness of time when God in Christ became man, human 'models' were giving us glimpses of divinity.

It seems strange therefore that earthy language about God and his behaviour is so often rejected as being too man-centred for theological accuracy, too anthropomorphic. "God bared his holy arm" is a scriptural commonplace yet abstract terms are felt to be more appropriate and "Our Father in heaven" fades into "The supreme spirit who alone exists of himself and is infinite in all his perfections." But really it is doubtful if technical terms can portray the original more faithfully than the language and lively antics of the living image and likeness. Even in their shame our first parents were telling us more about God our Creator than a world of abstract ideas.

So we look to our human-selves as a kind of blueprint or faint sketch of God and this would be fair enough but for the mysterious biblical phrase, "Let us make man in our own image and likeness". You would have expected in 'My image' or 'I shall make…' but there it stands, an enigma to the mono-theism of the Hebrews and so bafflingly expressed by an African proverb, "God is a majority of one."

If God is one how come this use of the plural long before the Christian revelation of the Trinity and long before a shamrock hinted at the mystery of three in one?

A model plane revealed many secrets of the real thing but can the created 'image and likeness', a human being, reflect a mystery such as this – one God speaking but in the language of 'us/we'; using the plural where we might have expected the singular, 'I/Myself'. Any answer springing from the human 'image' level would have to encompass some notion that included both the one and the many. It would have to hint at this paradox of the One God who yet speaks with the royal 'we'.

Well, "foxes have holes" and the "birds of the air have nests" and most of us have a family home – a place or grouping that is at once singular and plural. The number of our house may pin down our home to a single location but as soon as you enter the front door you are into plurality. Many persons, spouse, kids and relatives are there to greet you and you begin to see that the oneness of home is deeper than its simple location. Its unity is that of many persons living, through love, in one. Home tells of multiplicity bonded into unity by love and yet with one voice it speaks of 'we'. The family image and likeness of man, woman and child seems to be prophetic long before the full revelation of the Trinitarian good news by Christ. In his great priestly prayer (Jn 17) Jesus has perhaps conjured up for us the very roots of all that we call 'home'. In very simple language he prayed that, "They may all be one; even as thou, Father, art in me and I in thee, that they may also be in us…". It seems that home is a faint but dear image of that loving abiding of three Persons in One which gives to home all its precious associations. The Eastern Church reveres it as the 'circuminsession', that mystery wherein the divine Persons abide eternally each in the other; and such unity of love among many persons is perhaps the essence of what we call 'homeliness'.

So deep is the notion of home and family, with its strange admixture of the one and many, that it is invoked in every aspect of social life. There is a universal, ingrained desire to get together and form a whole out of many members. The United States, the late Soviet Union together with kingdoms and dictatorships all claim, by their very names, this family unity-in-plurality. Lower down in the social scale you find firms, clubs and co-ops all protesting their unity despite a membership that might extend as wide as the commonwealth itself. Who has not heard of Manchester United? Nothing seems able to disinfect the human heart of this notion of the one and the many, of unity and pluralism.

St Augustine made the daring claim that all things, not just human beings, seek to be united, to be at home. They are 'universed'; turned towards the one. Stones fall to their place of rest and it is said that even anchored battleships nudge together in a kind of affectionate bond, making a home of the harbour. It does begin to look as if all the fragments of creation are seeking the unity and multiplicity that is so evocative of the Trinity. But

Tho' we are many, we are one body & tho' there one bread.

home is special. It is composed of people and people are persons, profound, individual and mysterious; yet nothing seems to disinfect the human heart of this yearning for the one and the many, for unity in pluralism.

One of the most striking resemblances between home and its Origin or Exemplar is the equality of the three persons that make up the basic family structure. In the garden of Eden man and woman, were clearly on an equal footing as companions and helpmates – something that is coming over loud and clear in current feminist circles. More unexpected, perhaps, is the equal dignity of the parents and the child, with its mental and physical immaturity. You find this reflected in the laws of our own society where murder is murder without distinction of man, woman or child. There is a basic equality of persons in the human triad as in its Exemplar where three Persons are equal and united by love in one. To watch a family walking down the road, the child holding hands with parents on either side, is to glimpse a living image of the Trinity itself – three persons of one created nature bonded into a living and loving unity. Maybe this unity of the family is even more forcibly expressed in the home which, for all that it is a majority of one, is yet a communion of equal persons with love for its binding and driving force.

From films and novels it might seem that two is company and three is none for children seldom stray into romantic paperbacks. It was the great St Basil who insisted that the perfection of love is achieved

Our hearts are restless until they find their rest in thee

21

only in a triad where the mutual love of two persons is fulfilled in a 'condilectus', a 'co-loved one'. This is a third person who loves and is beloved by the pair. And from experience we all know the exclusiveness of a honeymoon couple, so wrapped up in themselves as to be oblivious of others, to the point of resenting normal communications. The room may be crowded to bursting but they have eyes only for each other and it takes the arrival of the child for the full cycle of mature love to emerge. Here parents love each other, love the child and the child is clearly barmy on both. The 'condilectus', the third person of the child has drawn the exclusive gaze of lovers to a world wider than their own small two-some and in so doing their love and society have become enriched.

There is a curious echo of this twosome love in the opening verses of the Fourth Gospel where you get the impression that Hollywood is right, with its 'two's company, three's none,' for St John seems to limit the divine exemplar to two, not three Persons in One. "In the beginning was the Word and the Word was with God..." But it is no accident that his Gospel is the Gospel of the Spirit of Love, of that mysterious Go-between third Person "whom the Father will send in my name", another comforter – exemplar, perhaps, of the 'condilectus'. Dualism does not reign in the Trinity any more than it should in the family. In fact, in the third world it is very moving to find how a childless marriage instinctively causes great sadness and is felt to be a social disaster. Third-worlders, more than Europeans, sense that the biological differences between man and woman clearly designate an expectancy of a third, the child. Its non-arrival is widely felt to be a shameful defect and a cause of much sorrow. They grieve for the lack of a 'condilectus', the third and beloved child. It is a lament for a triune unity.

Thus far, home and family have suggested something of the truth of those primordial words, "Let us make man in our own image and likeness". Home seems to reflect the Creator's oneness by virtue of the love that should bond its members into unity and something of this divine archetype is glimpsed in the global affirmation that "there is no place like home". But home is also a many personed affair with the triad of father, mother and child as the basic family structure. They are equal in dignity, sharing the same one nature, yet each is unique as a person and in the representative role of parent or child. A description of the family begins to read like the catechism on the Trinity where, "There are three persons in God: God the Father, God the Son and God the Holy Spirit." It begins to look as if the image and likeness of Genesis is speaking mysterious volumes.

16/8/04
Much of this calls to mind conversations yrs. ago when we questioned whether we WANTED a child and considered how bleak was Aylwyn & Lou's life without children
Consider US now wi. Fiona looking well set to bec. our dau-

23

3

The Child

Likenesses between the three divine Persons, in the unity of the Trinity and the family do not seem to stop at the mystery of the one and the many. Each person of the human triad, father, mother and child appears to resemble one of the divine Persons with almost uncanny fidelity. Surprisingly enough this is the powerful message of the child. The paradox of infancy evoking the Infinite is tough enough but juxtaposition of the child with the Third Person of the Trinity, the Holy Spirit, seems at first sight hopelessly inappropriate. Can 'image and likeness' really be taken so far as to compare an invisible, divine Person with the average chubby child? And yet reflection reveals some curious associations between such a child and the Spirit of Love.

Once again my own thoughts were sparked off by the strange ambivalence of literary language and symbol. I used to wonder why, of all things, pagan literature should designate a child as the god of love. Here in the classics, was the boy Cupid with his bow and arrow, setting hearts on fire. This seemed strange for romantic love is usually concerned with mature age rather than childhood and the last thing desired by lovers sitting on a park bench would be the presence of a small and inquisitive lad. Courtship is usually a private affair in which children are neither seen nor heard. Why then this curious choice of a child for the god of love?

C S Lewis had a theory that the old pagan myths had somehow cottoned on to deep intuitions about the Christian mysteries and were even at times prophetic. But the child Cupid seemed to defy his thesis for lovers are as a rule grown-ups. After all, the inspiration of so much poetry and song, from the courtly love of the Middle Ages to the present day, has been centred on an adult and bewitching lady love.

Gradually it dawned on me that the wisdom of the ages had not failed in its prophetic role by choosing Cupid as its god of love for the associations of childhood and the mystery of the Spirit are, in fact, very close. St Thomas Aquinas, a prince among theologians, has described the Holy Spirit as that Person of the Blessed Trinity who proceeds, by the spiration or breathing of love, from two other Persons as from a single principle. Such is his stammering presentation of the Spirit who in some strange way baffles our imagination.

And now, consider the child. Its description matches almost word for word those of St Thomas and its many associations seem to chime with our

CF. The Dancing Bear — where Holy John uses relationship betw. Sillo, Ariadne & the Bear to illustr. the Trinity.

basic theology of the Spirit. In St Thomas's description you could substitute 'child' for 'person' in almost every case. The child, imaging the procession of the Holy Spirit, proceeds from the two other persons of its parents so mutually united as to suggest a single principle. After all, Jesus himself tells us that the two shall become one flesh. "This is *our* new baby" they proudly say. Furthermore, the small bundle is also telling us that its origins, like those of the Spirit, were inspired by love and in different languages you often hear it called precisely a 'love-child'. True to its Trinitarian role, its response is that spontaneous return of affectionate love to both parent-persons so characteristic of children and so evocative of the Spirit. The child is at once a beloved and a loving person and the circle of human love, imaging the divine triad, is thus complete. Love binds the parents to this third person of the child, the 'condilectus', the 'co-loved one', and its return of love to them binds all three in one. No wonder that doting parents will give their child a name so reminiscent of the Spirit – 'Dorothy', or 'Matthew', which both mean the 'gift of God'; the very same name given by the Church to the Holy Spirit.

Curiously enough the newly arrived child adds a new and symbolic dimension to the meaning of our word 'neuter'. The infant in arms nearly always provokes the question, "What is *it*?" – a boy or a girl – since plump features give no hint of masculine or feminine identity. The message from the pram is not boy or girl but the neutrality of 'It' because for a few brief weeks masculine and feminine are, at face value literally indistinguishable. It is a case not of 'either/or' but of 'both and' which gives neutrality a sense of richness beyond its usual sense of deprivation. So we ask of a new baby, "What is *it*?" and the answer is that it is a two-in-one person who is showing us the mingled love and characteristics of its parents, the two persons from whence it has proceeded as if they were a single principle. Infancy confers upon our dead-sounding 'neuter' the dignity of its origin in those two persons whose combined love constituted it as a 'We person'.

It looks as if the infant is a kind of coded statement about the Spirit who is the Person of the Trinity proceeding from the Father and the Word. It seems very appropriate, therefore, that it is through the Holy Spirit that spiritual childhood should be conferred upon us.

According to St Paul it is the Holy Spirit who makes us cry out, "Abba, Father." But there seems to be more to it than that. At the last supper Jesus insisted on the 'witness' role of the Spirit – "he will bear witness to Me". The Spirit comes, not to reveal new truths, but to recall, to bear witness to, all that the Father has revealed through his Son. "He will bring to mind all that I have said to you." And this is perhaps a fundamental aspect of the child. It is a living witness to the existence and life of two other persons. On seeing a child wandering about looking lost, we instinctively ask, "Where are its mum and dad?" The child is plain testimony to its

two-personed origins and the welcome it gets when
restored to them is further evidence that it is a
beloved bond of union in the family triad. Witness
to its origins is almost the essence of childhood –
its mere presence testifying to its parents.

In Africa, more than in the West, you are more
conscious of another role of this small 'image and
likeness'. The child has a prophetic role that calls
to mind the Creed's declaration that the Spirit has
"spoken through the prophets". The African will
voice an almost embarrassing sympathy to a childless couple or even to an unmarried adult. And
behind this genuine concern lies the regret that
their lineage has come to a dead end with no promise of being perpetuated through the lives of children. The child is seen as prophetic of unending
family and tribal life. Such a promise of life gener-
ates joy and this is one of the fruits of the Spirit and
is usually characteristic of the child and its parents.
To the African mentality, especially, the lack of
offspring is a shadow of death that darkens joy.
Prophetic life is missing and with it the joyful hope
for the future of family and clan.

Furthermore, the Spirit is life-giving and children are nothing if not bursting with life. The
elderly couple next door to us finally moved out
when our large family moved into the adjoining
house. The very thought of so much spontaneous
and uninhibited vitality was too much for them.
Many grandparents today have to suppress similar
inclinations. Oddly enough the comedy and play-
fulness of children seems to echo the unexpected

humour of the Spirit spattering the pages of the Bible and of life itself. Samson ranks among his prophets yet some of his antics would earn high ratings on the box. St Peter, the heavenly door-keeper, is left knocking on John Mark's door, de-serted by the maid Rhode, too excited to open to him. Chesterton, in a moving passage, reckons that, in the final analysis, mirth is at the heart of the Blessed Trinity. Godhead, three in one, begins to sound like a kind of playground awaiting the en-trance of those who become joyful children of God.

When all is said and done, you could almost depict the child and its upbringing by the fruits of the Holy Spirit as if there were some mysterious affinity between the Paraclete and the children of Adam and Eve. Love and joy, there in plenty; patience often; gentleness, kindness and goodness are their due ambience and even that shy modesty that so befits well-brought-up children. It must be admitted however that self-control is not always so obvious in their teacup storms. It is consoling to reflect that, under grace, they usually grow up into the poise of mature childhood, like the boy Jesus.

To sum up 'image and likeness' help us to pen-etrate a little the mysterious association of the child with the Holy Spirit for both are witnesses to two other living and loving persons. The child's pro-phetic role is to give hope to its parents that their line will not die out and this is a hint and promise of eternal life, the gift of the 'Promise' of God, as an old hymn names the Spirit. St Thomas told us that the Spirit proceeds by way of spiration of love from two divine Persons and this might be a faithful description of the basic family unit where ideally the child is born of mutual parental love and becomes the bond between them. The saint, in fact, might have been describing the primeval notion of home as the abode of many persons, of the one human nature, united in love as one. It is no wonder that we grown-ups grow thoughtful at those simple words, "Unless you become as little children, you cannot enter the kingdom of God". Yet hope does not desert us for the Spirit has been sent precisely to convince us and console us in the knowledge that we 'really are children of God'.

4

Show Us the Father

blowoth where .r hoto h

There is a certain elusiveness about the Holy Spirit whom Jesus likened to the wind. The child, too, behaves with something of the same baffling freedom and spontaneity. It is then with relief that we learn from Jesus to call God 'Our Father'. We feel at home with the notion of fatherhood since it is a relationship which so many have known and loved. And in a single verse St Paul makes it easy for us to rise from the human image and likeness to that of our heavenly 'Abba'. "For this reason I fall on my knees before the Father from whom every family in heaven and on earth receives its true name". St Paul was in fact echoing a theme dear to the heart of Christ – "If you then who are evil know how to give good gifts to your children, how much more will your heavenly Father give the Holy Spirit to those who ask him". Jesus is impressing on us the existence of a heavenly Father whose concern reminds us of earthly fathers with gratitude and joy.

Fathers, for example, are at the origin of our human existence, the source of our human lives and as such they are shadowing the Father who is the eternal origin of life in the Blessed Trinity. As if to emphasise this mysterious affinity we talk of the 'procreation' of children and the word is reminiscent of the Father's creative action in bringing us and the universe into being. After all, authentic human fatherhood is basically a manifestation of goodness overflowing in a gift that bears its own living likeness; and that resonates powefully with the inner dynamic of the trinity. We follow this up by praying, as Jesus taught us, "Give us this day our daily bread" because fathers, heavenly or human, do just that. Having given us life they go on to sustain it by the gift of life-giving food. Fatherhood is an ongoing process and we begin to realise just what the Father does for us as we recall the untiring concern of so many fathers to provide the clothing and shelter that enabled us to live. The eternal Father hopes to see us grow into the family image and likeness of his only Son just as our human fathers hope that their children will grow freely into the attitudes and assumptions they themselves hold dear. It begins to dawn that the human love which fathered us into existence is but a reflection of the stance towards us of the God who is love. Like the divine archetype, our own fathers desired nothing more than a return of grateful love, the most longed for response of fathers, heavenly or human. Significantly the 'Eucharist', which is at the heart of Christianity, means 'thanksgiving'.

But when Jesus comes to speak explicitly of his Father at the Last Supper, things get very mysterious. Philip asked him a very simple question and hoped for a simple answer that would satisfy his deepest longings as well as ours. "Lord show us the Father – that is all we ask." But the reply baffled him as much as it baffles us. "He who has seen me has seen the Father... do you not believe that I am in the Father and the Father is in me?" One Person spoke these mysterious words but he expected Philip to see, or to realise, the presence of two, "He who has seen me has seen the Father". How on earth can you see two distinct persons in the single one standing before you? Even the great proving works of Jesus, his miracles of healing and of raising the dead, seemed unable to convince the apostles that Jesus was speaking plain fact – "He who has seen me has seen the Father".

I doubt if anyone will ever plumb those strange Trinitarian words but not long ago I got a curious insight into their actuality. Two of us were standing outside the monastery guest house and I was asking my actor friend if it was difficult to maintain his identity, to remember who he really was after a lifetime of playing so many roles. And while I was talking, suddenly he disappeared; he just was not there and creepily I found myself face to face with a stooped and melancholic stranger. An abrupt, uncanny chill gripped me until my friend, laughingly dropped the role of Hamlet he had suddenly assumed. "Yes," he admitted, "character roles can so possess you that at times you must struggle to find your real self." It had been a superb piece of acting in which he had seemed to disappear and Hamlet, as real as life, had stood before me.

"He who has seen me has seen the Father", said Jesus and Philip was baffled by the paradox of looking at Jesus and being asked to see the Father. Now my friend had demonstrated in chilling fashion that one person could vanish and yet still be present, though hidden, in the features and personality of another. He had never left me but he had so emptied himself of his own characteristics as to reveal those of another. I was seeing Hamlet and yet was present to my friend. One person was revealing a second. All that, of course, was make-believe; a living mask of a famous character but maybe it hinted at a profound Trinitarian mystery.

It goes, perhaps, like this. Christ, the Word, is the Icon, the Image of God – a living mirror image, so to speak, of the infinite, eternal Father. He is 'ad Patrem'; facing the Father'. Now the special property of a mirror is to reveal with great fidelity what stands before it. A good mirror, like a good actor, remains invisible behind its role and yet is always present. Have you ever sat in a mirror-walled restaurant and wondered at its spaciousness and if those tables far off are real or not? Both mirror and actor have emptied themselves of all but what they reflect. And Jesus, the Image Incarnate of God, has emptied himself of divine manifestations to do on earth what he, as the eternal Image and Word, has been doing from all eternity – revealing and mirroring the Father.

An actor can startle us with the realism of his assumed role even though it is make-believe. But in the dynamic of the Trinity "All I have is yours, Father" and that hints at an effacement of self that totally reveals the beloved Father. It is no assumed role but an infinite mirror image, invisible in its activity of perfect reflection, though personally never absent. "He who sees me sees the Father."

And when the Image became flesh, one of us, the Person of the Word lost none of its Trinitarian dynamic. Jesus, the Word Incarnate stands before us but is revealing, as in eternity, the Father. It is an activity of self-emptying, a loving kenosis. He is doing what the Word has always been doing – reflecting "the glory of God and bearing the very stamp of his nature" (cf. Heb 1:3). As the Jerusalem Bible notes, "He is the replica of the Father's substance, like an exact impression made by a seal on clay or wax".

In a hopelessly inadequate sense, you could say that Jesus, like a supreme actor, so empties and effaces himself in revealing his Father that he seems to vanish as did my actor friend. When reading the gospels many of us perhaps imagine the Father as being in heaven whilst his Son treads this dusty earth far removed though somehow united with his Father in the Person and love of the Spirit. But Jesus is true God and not just true man for "in him all the fullness of God was pleased to dwell". Presence to Jesus is presence to the Father. Such was his assurance to Philip's anxious question... "Do you not believe that I am in the Father and the

Father is in Me?" Christ, the Word made flesh, is doing on earth what the Word has ever been doing in heaven. Perhaps we see in the face on the Turin shroud a mirror of the Father's anguish and the mysterious cost to the Blessed Trinity of restoring the image and likeness of God, lost at the Fall.

In my friend I saw Hamlet yet my friend was still before me. I looked at one person but two seemed present. Philip looking at Christ was assured that he was seeing the Father. And what of our own anxious prayer, "Show us the Father"? Well, "Who has seen me has seen the Father." If the family home is a faint icon of the unity of the Trinity and if the human triad of father, mother and child is a created manifestation of the divine Persons, then we begin to see that human fathers can help us to see our heavenly Father for many have tried to live out their role as 'image and likeness' with extraordinary fidelity. In time, they brought us into life and by their work fostered that life with food, roof, and clothing. They gave us a loving example of the rights and responsibilities of being human and did all this to prepare us for the everlasting fatherhood that awaits us in heaven. Jesus revealed to us his Father and fathers can, by their Christlike spirit, try to do no less for us.

5

The Woman You Gave Me

If in some mysterious way the basic family triad of man, woman and child is a created image and likeness of the Blessed Trinity then we begin to wonder what has happened to the resemblance between the woman and one of the divine Persons. Christ through constant reiteration has made the father image plain beyond doubt and the child shows remarkable affinity with the love-inspired procession of the Holy Spirit but little is said about 'mother'. Feminists are indignant that the theology of womanhood has been almost totally neglected and they ask just why the child in the manger was a boy and not a girl. They wonder at the plain facts of history which tell us that the Word became a man, not a woman.

This brings me back to that course in English literature alerting me to the ambivalence of language. It was constantly using sacred and heavenly terms for earthly love situations. Sylvia, you may remember, was 'adorable' and Cleopatra's perfections were 'infinite'. This however was not too puzzling for we were made in the 'image and likeness' of God. A model behaves and speaks to a limited extent like its original which explains why sacred and profane language can be so easily transposed. Image theology came to the rescue and once again it was through a lived experience that I began to glimpse the nature of womanhood as image of and likeness to its Trinitarian origins.

This time it was as guest father in an African monastery where for years I had been giving retreats to religious sisters and lay women but was doing so with a growing sense of frustration. Centuries of male orientated spirituality were there to guide me but they seemed to offer little that was specifically feminine. St Ignatius was at your side in a flash, with his soldiers of Christ battling away and there was St Teresa of Avila constantly urging her daughters to be courageous and strong like men. As a retreat giver I seemed to be taking the same line, using the same stereotypes of combat, initiative and mastery of faults. All of which added up to a kind of masculine ethic rather than an organic spiritual life rooted in the nature of womanhood.

In looking for a theology of the feminine one seemed to be baffled from the start by the usual presentation of God himself (sic) as predominantly masculine. In the Old Testament he is Lord of Hosts and in the Gospels we think almost exclusively of our Heavenly Father or of the Word made flesh in the man Jesus Christ. There seemed little incentive to look for a theology of womanhood in

One so evidently masculine. On the other hand, paganism never seems to let the matter rest and its deep-rooted aspirations for a goddess, such as Diana of the Ephesians, are persistent enough to suggest a human need answering in some way to reality.

Yet curiously enough the Word of God, the Second Person who came as man, has long biblical associations with womanhood. In the Book of Proverbs, Feminine Wisdom greets with smiling face the friends of God and according to chapter eight, She is there at the beginnings of creation as a kind of helpmate to the Lord. One verse from the prophet Baruch (ch 3; v 37), startlingly prophetic, states bluntly that "afterwards SHE appeared upon earth and lived among men." The theme also runs through the *Book of Wisdom* whose author seems intent on creating an aura of divine and feminine personhood with almost Trinitarian overtones. She is a "spotless mirror of the working of God and image of his goodness". She "reaches mightily from one end of the earth to the other and She orders all things well". *The New Jerusalem Bible* in a footnote to the first verse of St John's Gospel refers to this 'Word-Wisdom' as a person whom John describes as 'with', facing the Father. In that eternal stance of the Word we seem to glimpse the 'She', the very archetype of woman's being. Mother Julian works this up into a veritable theology, appropriating to Jesus, the Word Incarnate, all the attributes of womanhood. Julian does it with a few crisp sentences. "So we see that Jesus is the true Mother of our nature, for he made us. He is our Mother, too, by grace because he took our created nature upon himself. All the lovely deeds and tender services that beloved motherhood implies are appropriate to the Second Person."

One of the reasons why theologians are wary of such a theology is the outmoded assumption that woman's role is passive and therefore incapable of imaging the Word since there can be no passivity in God. Behind such thought is the notion that feminine receptivity is purely passive whereas receptivity need be no more passive than masculine donation. This is something that we see very clearly if we think in terms of 'welcome'. There is a huge difference between an active, outgoing welcome of a guest and the frigid passivity which marks the reception of the proverbial poor relation! Receptivity becomes active, dynamic, as soon as it is inspired by love. Its dignity in the Trinity, as in human relations, is equal to that of donation or giving.

Even in the important area of motherhood a woman's potentiality for parenting springs from this innate charism of 'active receptivity', something which is stamped on her whole person as being in the image and likeness of the Eternal Word. In a limited sense a man may be characterised by the active gift of self in fatherhood which comes to fruition in the child, whilst in an equally limited sense a woman may be characterised by the active reception of life which she then returns to the father in the child – a gift cared for, enriched and given back.

In all of this the notions of active donation and active receptivity play their equal and complementary roles, even as in the Word, there is no hint of passivity but only the archetype of all receiving and giving in love. This active receptivity is then a charism that finds its powerful expression in both spiritual and human motherhood – a charism, so to speak, of welcome.

Such an interpretation of motherhood might be dismissed as poetic license yet Mother Julian steadily insists on the motherhood of Christ. It is so emphatic and is drawn out with such theological precision that it is hard to see it as devotional language or metaphor. To Julian it comes across as dogmatic fact. "As truly as God is our Father, so just as truly is he our Mother," or "In our Father, God Almighty, we have our being; in our merciful Mother Christ we are remade and restored..." "So Jesus Christ who sets good against evil is our real Mother. We owe our being to him – and this is the essence of motherhood and all the delightful, loving protection which ever follows." Finally she wraps it all up in a Trinitarian formula. "Hence it follows that God is as truly our Mother as he is our Father. Our Father decides, our Mother works, our good Lord, the Holy Spirit, strengthens." Julian's theology seems to express, with feminine insight and empathy, the cold dogma of the manuals that relations of opposites best describe the relationship of Father and Word in the love of the Spirit.

If then every family in heaven and on earth receives its true name from the Father, then it looks as if every mother receives her true identity from the Word, the Icon of the Father and the Second Person of the Blessed Trinity. Historically, this Word came among us as 'true man', as totally male, because the Word's person from eternity has always been to reflect and reveal the Father.

Nevertheless, the Person behind the eyes of Christ is the Wisdom Word, whom all femininity mirrors in created fashion. But like a supreme actor, the Word's revelation of the Father is so mirror-perfect as to conceal the divine personhood. This does not imply any notion of gender in the Godhead but the created image and likeness in men and women is telling us a great deal about our mysterious and triune origin. There is an added bonus. There can be no inequality between the sexes for their true basis of equality is imaging that of the Father, Word and Holy Spirit – a fact that should end forever the squabbling between us. One question though remains. How reconcile the feminine associations of the Word, the Second Person of the Trinity, with the man our Lord and Saviour Jesus Christ?

6

Christ Our Mother

Julian, of course, has not enlarged upon the burning issue that seems to call in question her endearing theology of the motherhood of Christ. If Jesus came among us as a man, how call him 'mother'; how come this association with motherhood and femininity?

I can still remember discussing this objection with a nun at the grill of a Carmelite convent. "Why should the Word, the Wisdom of God become man, not woman?" And I can recall how the response sprang simultaneously to our lips. "Because Jesus is the total revelation of the Father." His great passion was to show us his Father. It took me a long time to work out the implications of that mutual intuition.

Jesus himself constantly tells us that he has come to reveal the Father in those words already quoted, "He who has seen me has seen the Father". He does this with the single-mindedness of a lover wanting to make known to others their beloved even at the cost of total self-abnegation. The Word is the full expression of the Father's being and the Word now made flesh would continue this expression, not only by word and deed, but by assuming the very lineaments of human manhood. If there is something in man that is appropriated to the Father then the Word made flesh comes to reveal him to us, even bodily. The Word, from all eternity, has been "the full expression of his being" and now in time this shines through in the man Jesus Christ.

We know that Jesus is true God and true Man but perhaps we forget that he has no human personality simply because it is the divine Person of the Word who looks out from his human eyes. St Peter, in the early days, thought he was walking alongside the person of an attractive human friend. Only later came the shattering revelation that this was "The Son of the Living God" and no mere carpenter from Nazareth. His friend was, in fact, a divine Person showing us, in a perfect human nature, his Father.

The curious thing is that you often catch overtones of this Person in the Gospels and they are powerfully evocative of womanhood. For instance, at a very human level Jesus shows an extraordinary affinity with woman. He is born of a virgin with no trace of man's intervention and infinitely tender to women in all strata of society. The street sinner, weeping at his feet, goes home justified; he alone refuses to condemn the woman taken in adultery and to the astonishment of the apostles, he, a Jew, is found chatting to a woman at the well-side – and she a Samaritan. His sharp eye does not miss the two copper coins of the widow's mite and the prayer of two sisters moves him to bring back Lazarus from the dead. Women minister to him on the roads and at journey's end. He would gather Jerusalem to himself like a mother her chicks. In the upper room he prays that we may make our home in him and there, like any housewife, he is concerned to prepare a meal. Here, from the gift of his very flesh and blood we seem to catch overtones of the hidden nourishment of the unborn child by the flesh and blood of the mother. This perhaps suggests a natural and maternal basis for the Eucharist which water's washing gives to Baptism and oil's unction to Confirmation. In the early Church a martyr's death was often heralded as his '*dies natalis*', his birthday from this earthly life into eternal life. In like fashion Christ mothers us on earth with his flesh and blood until we, too, are born into the light of eternity. Moreover '*Christus lactans*', nourishing humanity from his pierced side, is a very ancient devotion still alive in theological journals and it seems to encapsulate this very thought. Even from the cross, where women were at the forefront, he is anxious to provide a home for his mother and it was to women that he first revealed himself after the resurrection. No wonder Julian called him 'Christ my Mother'. Mothers conceal and then reveal the hidden person within them and this is a faint shadowing of the mystery of the Incarnate Word dwelling among us, the one Person hiddenly revealing the presence of another. Jesus emphatically is true man and everything about him speaks to us of the Father and of manhood but he is also the Person of the Word and in him the glorious associations of womanhood keep on breaking out.

Maybe one of Mary's greatest prerogatives is that she is telling us of her Son's divine and mysterious personality. She may be revealing to us in human fashion and through all the facets of her womanhood all that the Father would have us know of his Word, 'Lady Wisdom'. But her Son's task is to reveal the Father. Despite the fact that he is the second Person, the Word to whom womanhood seems to correspond, this in no way clashes with the fact that the Word assumes human nature as a man. For the Word is ever the perfect revelation of the Father, and Jesus manifests this in radical body language.

Here we have come full circle, back to our basic text, "Let us make man in our own image and likeness". Significantly it goes on, "Male and female he created them." If a statue projects the image of its original and if creation is stamped with the image of the Triune God then it is hard to escape the conclusion that both man and woman represent, in their created way, his image and likeness. Or to put it the other way round, perhaps the shortest description of the Trinity would be 'Two Persons in Love,' the eternal archetype of the family triad.

And what comes of all this? Surely an orientation, if not a basis, for a spirituality more in conformity with a woman's nature than the usual adaptations of a masculine ethic. If the theology of the Word is really built into the very structure of woman and if woman really is in the image and likeness of God in body, psyche and soul, then it becomes possible to drop much of the 'spiritual warrior' type of spirituality. It becomes possible to work out the implications in very simple guidelines. "Be what you are, a woman, the icon of the Word and actively live out the glorious implications of this fact." Jesus, the man, is for all humans the only Way, Truth and Life but women can gaze with special understanding into the depths of his divine personality and see in this Wisdom-Word an abandonment to the Father and concern for others that speaks to the very roots of their being. At this point one could draw out all the implications of such a guideline and range from woman's lib to a rationale of cosmetics but here one can only give a few pointers.

Where start? Perhaps with what is most immediately to hand, namely with our bodies for they are a kind of sacrament, an outward sign of our deepest being and orientation. The body bears the image of the Trinity that is stamped on our souls and psyche – even as the image and likeness is stamped on all creation. A woman's whole structure carries the special imprint of the Word who is the Divine Life actively received and returned in love as totally as it is given. Such a concern for other persons is almost the hallmark of life in the Trinity.

And so a woman is appropriately built to welcome, carry and protect a life other than her own. She is 'mother of the living' both physical and spiritual and the womb and breast have become the symbols of all that nurtures and fosters life, a life that must grow ultimately to the fully autonomous person of the child. Even bodily, she is telling us of the Word who is 'concerned' to receive from the Father the gift of life and give it back embellished in the same Spirit of Love. Woman, the icon of the Word, receives in motherhood a life other than her own and now gives it back enhanced in perfect childhood to the father.

Then the roles are mutually reversed. Her reception has become donation as she bears the child to the father and his role has become active reception as he receives the child, his gift of life embellished, into his arms. All of which is a shadowy image of the perfect equality and mutual activity of the three divine Persons. It is also the whole thrust of the Word made flesh. Jesus came to give back to the Father lives other than his own through a total abandonment of his life to the Father – a mothering gesture of returning to a father the gift of life now revealed in us, the children.

If all such notions were boiled down into a single word, I imagine it would echo von Hugel's last poignant utterance. "It is caring that matters; caring matters most." And when you come to consider the deep roots of the Hebrew word for compassion and mercy you understand why caring had such affinity with one of woman's most endearing roles. 'Rachamim' in Hebrew has come to mean compassion because in the singular it can signify the womb, the place where long and silent care nurtures life. Basically the word seems to evoke the warm security of a nest where unremitting presence and warmth coax life into this world. In the final analysis 'racham' translates as 'woman', as if personalising all the associations of her femininity with its care, sympathy and concern. "If God were to touch you," said a lady therapist, "You might die of fright, but if he were to touch you through me, you might be consoled."

7

Two in One

One of the surprises of computer technology is the use of very human and sometimes endearing language in their handbooks. In the hi-tech world of microchips you hardly expect to find homeliness yet such manuals often read like a guide for earthly or eternal living. You may be asked to choose from a *menu* or hit the *home* key. If there is risk of a power cut you are advised to *save* your text at frequent intervals and if it does get lost there is always the assurance of salvation. It may be lingering in *limbo* whence it can be retrieved. Even the ultimate destiny of life is evoked in the possibility of text *justification* or of its *abandonment* for ever. High technology for all its cold precision grows almost folksy as its scientists now fall back on *fragrance* or *charm* as the most accurate descriptions of elusive sub-atomic particles. Science is at last beginning to shake hands with common humanity.

We learn from Genesis that God made us in his

image and likeness and it really begins to look as if we, in our turn, follow his example and fashion even computers in our own image and likeness. Basically though the trend is understandable. Just as a model plane imitates to some extent the real thing so we human images of God try to do likewise. All our activities shadow the inner dynamics of the Triune God and this copycat fact is crucial to an understanding of the most significant events of life – marriage, birth and death.

In St John's Gospel Jesus reveals divine life as an eternal game of self-giving, of gift and giving again. "All I have is yours, Father, and all you have is mine." The Father in Love gives himself totally to the Word and the Word returns such Love enhanced with the gift of Self. To our limited vision it all seems like an infinite ocean of mutual self-giving in which love reaches ever growing heights and depths with each ebb and flow of the tide.

And we the images would do the same for we also were made to give and receive. For example, the simple offer of a box of chocolates carries with it something of the gift of our selves. The joy and affection that it provokes in the other is a measure of increasing love as they in turn beam back their thanks to us. And all this is a shadow of the triune game of gift and giving again. It is a kind of dance in which all are invited to join and, when we come to marriage, resonances with Trinitarian dynamics reach a climax. Here we are in the realms of personal relations and, unlike computers, it is a world of memories, hopes, loves and fears.

Programmers may see us as a complex of electronic stimuli but a human father is more than a slot machine for pocket money and mother is more than a source of apple pie. In all our relationships the mysterious interplay of free will, the risks of mutual trust and the fruition of self-gift all crowd out the mechanical aspects of sheer supply and demand. "Do you take Ruth to be your wedded wife?" So runs the marriage formula and there follows a scary pause before the answer jolts us into the presence and seriousness of personal choice. Only after an eternity of seconds comes "I do".

All of which is a deeply Trinitarian dynamic answering to the eternal self-giving of person to person in a spirit of love. But the human imagery does not stop there. The old marriage rite went on to externalise this mutual self-gift in very human terms. "With my body I thee worship..." and in reckless abandon, "With all my worldly goods I thee endow." Vatican II may have changed the wording but the intention endures and echoes the very words of the Second Person of the Trinity, "All I have, is yours, Father, and all you have is mine". The marriage couple have pledged their lives, their bodies and finally their very possessions to each other in a union of love so close that Jesus' prayer seems to gather bridegroom and bride into the very heart of the Trinity. "Father may they be one in us as You are in me and I in You...".

An event so reminiscent of triune life is bound to reflect something of divine splendour and joy and we Westerners shower the happy couple with confetti whilst Easterners honour them with garland and crown. All the world loves a lover because the human image reflects a little of the beauty and bliss of its divine exemplar.

Heaven's happiness gladdens earth's weddings. We may object that Trinitarian likeness in fact falls short since only two persons, not three, walk to the altar. The third person, the image of the Spirit of Love, seems missing. Not really – an old custom puts aside the top tier of the wedding cake in the expectation of a christening and the third person is present in the promise of a child, the love child inspired by the love of two other persons.

The child is not only the seal of their mutual self-giving in love but it also shares the mysterious title of the Spirit whom Jesus calls the 'Promise' of the Father. A promise, after all, is built on expectation and hope for a child is the happy expectation of all at a wedding. Bride, groom and child are reminding us of the only true God, three Persons lovingly united in One.

The attractiveness of a good marriage is of course the mutual and lasting fidelity of husband and wife, caught up with the care of their children. There is something deeply impressive about a family celebration of a silver or golden jubilee and maybe it is because we are catching a glimpse of the permanent and eternal self-gift of Persons in the Trinity, a gift so total as to be irrevocable. Divine unending fidelity seems to point logically to the indissolubility of marriage and a jubilee is an echo of such loyalty. Instinctively we recoil from divorce for there is nothing more wounding than a gift given and then taken back.

You get an inkling of the tragedy of a marriage that has dissolved or broken down in the last hours of the crucifixion, "My God, my God why have you forsaken me?" For a moment it looked as if the eternal gift of Person to Person in Love had collapsed in the stress of suffering; as if Christ the Word Incarnate was being rejected by his Father. No wonder that the earth quaked and the sky grew dark when the Trinity itself seemed to be disintegrating and God forsaking God. That 'Eloi, Eloi' hinted at the awful blackout of abandonment by his Father and a kind of divine divorce seemed to hover over the cross. Christ had emptied himself and given all and death's isolation was the mocking response. But the Father, at the resurrection, did answer his desperate cry and raised him from death to life, for the ebb and flow of love and life between the Three Persons cannot fail. All basis for fidelity in marriage and human friendship could have crumbled but for the trusting fidelity of Jesus' "Into thy hands I commend my spirit". Trinitarian fidelity and marriage fidelity, like diamonds "are for ever" and we warm to the thought of newlyweds living happily ever after.

All of which may seem too rosy a view of marriage in the face of statistics assuring us that one in three breaks down and that marriage is steadily giving way to temporary commitments. Official forms no longer ask the name of husband or wife but of one's partner. Yet despite the prevailing climate of liberalism, a vague sense of uneasiness still prevails. It witnesses to Chesterton's contention that the one certain thing about the human race is that something has gone radically wrong. Daily the media confirms his thesis with endless presentations of crime, violence and divorce – of all that is the very antithesis of divine or human fidelity in marriage or close relationships.

Things would turn out differently if we lived true to the pattern of the Trinity where Persons are total 'givers' in an ambience of love. But to some extent we have all become 'grabbers' rather than 'givers' and this puts our lifelong commitments in personal relationships at risk. The ultimate term of grasping self-love is a kind of isolation that is perhaps the shadow of death – separation from God and from fellow human beings.

This kind of death scene could not reign in God since God is love and love, in eternity, like a long rally in tennis, swings back and forth in a rhythmic and life-giving 'now'. But with us, where time and succession rule, there is the chance to pause, hesitate and perhaps refuse love for love. We may feel the richer for hanging on to another's gift of themselves to us but if we make no response it will mean increasing isolation and loneliness. If the Trinity seems like a kind of 'giving machine' we, but for the grace of God, can become 'grabbing machines' heading for those harbingers of death – divorce, abortion, euthanasia and all that is life not lived in love. Grasping or giving make all the difference between the tensed atmosphere of a broken relationship or the warmth of a family where parents are united in their mutual love, personified in an affectionate child – a triad of mutual love.

One of the most persuasive indications of our Trinitarian resemblance is the persistent use of nuptial language in the writings of great saints as they attempt to describe the union of the soul with God. They see spiritual marriage as the climax of sanctity on earth and the underlying logic is not difficult. The inner dynamic of the Triune God is a total gift of Person to Person in the Spirit of Love. It is an eternal union of many persons in one and something Christ expressed so pithily, "The Father and I are one". Self-gift in love is the heart, so to speak, of the Trinity and it is not hard to see how marriage images this profound mystery and gives grounds for a spiritual interpretation. "Do you take him/her to be your wedded spouse?" And the "I do" clinches the mutual self-gift consummated in the union of "one flesh". A wedding unites two persons at every level, spiritual or physical, and hints at the saints' deepest longings for a union with God which nothing less than 'spiritual marriage' seems able to describe.

Perhaps especially significant in these days of feminist theology is the Creed's insistence on the equality of the divine Persons.

Jesus, the Word made flesh, is God from God, of one being with the Father. Marriage was meant to reflect this equality and in the home there is no room for male or female domination, not even for the tyranny of a difficult child. The human image and likeness was meant to be true to the equality of persons in its Trinitarian origins.

For all that, the persistent notion endures in so many cultures that the man should dominate family life; that the husband has the '*potestas patris*', that power of the father which in ancient Rome extended to the power of life and death even over a natural child.

Male domination seems to have threatened women from the start of the human race. It seems odd that only recently has it come under heavy and deserved fire, mostly in western cultures. And it is not only a very ancient phenomenon but also a global one. An African chief being told that Queen Victoria reigned over the then British Empire, retorted, "Can a monkey rule?" Worldwide, women are recruited for industry, not only for their deftness in repetitive work, but on the general assumption that they can be paid lower wages. They are simply more cost-effective. It is a grim story constantly repeated in history. Even in the Old Testament, on the rare occasions when women take centre stage, they may perform heroically but their real status in the community is betrayed by the Jewish morning prayer; the suppliant thanks God for making him a man, not a woman.

The Christian era seems to offer no respite and St Paul has become the *bete noire* of woman's lib. The wife should be subject to her husband who is the head of the wife as Christ is the head of the Church. Women should be silent in church and, perforce, wearing hats! It is only fair to redress the balance by recalling that St Paul's male domination is Christian only if it is expressed in loving service. "A husband must love his wife as his own body...", for to reign with Christ is to serve. Mutual loving service is the leitmotif of his letters and does something to level things out. Paul did realise that fatherly responsibility disinfects any hint of superiority – after all, Christ his Master washed the disciples' feet.

If the Church down the ages had heeded the spirit of such teaching the lid today would not have blown off so violently.

Centuries later the high and romantic courtesy of the Middle Ages helped to reverse the trend. The legendary knight vowed himself unto death to honour, protect and serve his 'lady love'. Dragons, hopeless quests and even scullery washing up were all at her service. Perhaps the twilight of such chivalry still illuminates the true nature of headship as service with 'ladies first' or the offer of a seat in the bus.

We may not be able to eradicate this long history of male domination but Christianity does at least expose its falsity and weaken its grasp. A father's headship is revealed as service in the family's best interests. Marriages are made in the glorious equality of the children of God and there, in heaven, they are meant to return to join in the Great Dance of triune and personal give and take.

8

Man's Lib

"You know," said a doctor friend, "I think that in this day and age men have lost their nerve." She was thinking of the fierce backlash to centuries of male domination, condensed into the modern assumption that 'men are chauvinistic pigs'. Perhaps these two-legged porkers are at last trying to redress the balance and, after all, both St Teresa of Avila and St Catherine of Siena have been made Doctors of the Church and Thérèse of Lisieux has now followed suit. There is no doubt that the flood tide of women's lib is sweeping in and confidence is so high that a word or two about men, for all their bad press, may just be tolerated.

So far, we have seen that we are created in the likeness of the Triune God, so that our mirroring image as men and women should bear some resemblance to the dignity and equality of the three Persons. Scripture, Creed and Tradition are uncompromising in declaring this absolute equality. "The Word was with God and the Word was God..."

This is the same Wisdom-Person, who became flesh and categorically affirmed his divinity, "before Abraham was, I am". His claim to know the Father and to be the only one fully known by him implies an equality that is echoed in the Creed's "consubstantial with the Father", whilst the Holy Spirit "is with the Father and the Son worshipped and glorified". From such compelling evidence of equality in the Trinity we gain some hope of finding its counterpart between the sexes. Woman's lib really should equate with man's but we live in this world of time where things have a beginning and an end, and temporal things are caught up into a pecking order with origins at the top. Vintage cars have an enduring dignity, old houses are listed and the family patriarch is traditionally given the place of honour. The man, Adam, was the first to walk in Eden and he seems to have claimed priority ever since.

Not so in the Godhead where there is no time, no before and after, only the eternal 'now'. It is an ever present moment beyond our powers of understanding or description. Scripture and theology tell us that the Father gives himself totally in the generation of the Word in Love and that the Word, in this 'now', is total self-gift to the Father. We would conclude that the Father is in some way superior because he 'first' has the gift of Self to bestow. In our time conditioned world we feel indebted and almost inferior to even the kindliest of benefactors for they already have the means to supply what we lack. But in the eternal 'now' the gift is simultaneously given back and, in the Trinity, there reigns an instantaneous and everlasting equality. We flick on the light switch and the light bulb gives out light to the whole room but is itself revealed in the light, instantaneously reflected back. Light and its reflection are simultaneous and coequal. In the Trinity there is no question of priority for the Word is "God from God, Light from Light, True God from True God." Fatherhood there claims no dominance nor superiority and this is the true exemplar of equality between man and woman, male and female, husband and wife.

We however are time conditioned and things are different. A sense of superiority creeps in because the very notion of giving life through fatherhood implies possession in the donor and some form of poverty in the recipient, awaiting alleviation. Our kindliest intentions are fraught with a lurking sense of patronage since, having something to give, we are threatened with the risk of becoming patronising. This helps to explain the long association of superiority with origins and maybe underlies the myth that fathers and men in general are pre-eminent by right. Biblical tradition, though, goes deeper than this, suggesting that things fell apart almost from the beginning when the mutual partnership of gender equality deteriorated into lordship and subjection. With the apple, male chauvinism became a possibility. Man and woman tried to grab it from God and nothing so alienates as theft from a kindly friend. Alienation from God only leads to alienation from his image and likeness, not only between the sexes but wherever his image is found. Alienation of man from woman follows and spills over to murder in the next generation as Cain kills Abel and creation bares its fangs in thorns until nature becomes red in tooth and claw. Domination by force has supplanted the mutual equality of loving service in the game of give and give again. Giving has yielded to grabbing. Since the man usually has the greater physical strength, male domination in such a climate steadily intensifies. A hideous state of affairs, though in all fairness it must be admitted that feminine manipulation comes a close second to man's tyranny and is perhaps its match!

The pathos of all this is that male chauvinistic piggery is really the distorted mirror image of what maleness is all about. Expressed in terms of fatherhood, the man, imaging the divine exemplar, is the human source of life and this too is an initiative or origin that carries with it no superiority. Despite all the salacious jokes in the world he is the seed-bearer, the one whose dignity is to carry the seed essential to the continuance of the race. In this and in the procreation of his own image and likeness, man's sexuality is but one aspect of our shadowing the Trinity, perhaps the most powerful and the most fraught with danger. Ideally sexuality is the equal self-gift of two human persons in love, inspiring the being of a third person in the child – three persons of equal dignity united in the one nature of which home is so compelling a symbol. This gives no licence for so-called 'free love' for where self-gift is total there can be no fragmentation of the gift, no repudiation. A total free gift is non-negotiable. Married love was meant to be for ever and its permanence gives us a glimpse of the eternal bond within the Triune God.

Man, then, carries with him this profound mystery of the seeds of his own image and this gives rise to a notion of origins and initiative that risks a sense of domination. Semen, however, is not superior to the ovum and the man's life-giving and life-imaging role of fatherhood is void without the equally essential role of woman's motherhood. Their dignity was designed to be mutual partnership with one as the instigator and provider of life whilst the other is its bearer and intimate carer. The only difference in such mutual activity, important to a later consideration of sacrifice, is that the male bestows, hands over, parts with something already possessed. He has a gift to bestow, the seeds of his own living image and likeness. This may seem to imply superiority but is balanced totally by the return of the gift, now enhanced, in the new born child. Donation is crowned by fruitful and active receptivity.

It may well be objected that to equate masculine and feminine simply in terms of biological function is a singularly limited view of human potentiality – what of our great musicians, poets and painters; what of our Florence Nightingales and Leonard Cheshires? What of the infinite number of skills that grace both men and women, married or single? Furthermore, St Augustine discerned the Trinitarian image, not in gender characteristics, but in our nobler endowments of memory, intellect and will. These are valid objections but the pattern of the Trinitarian self-gift of Persons in love is stamped on us body as well as soul. The physical character-istics of male and female are manifestly designed for self-gift in a union of love. And this gift of sexuality, for all its abuses, clearly proclaims the complementarity and equality of man, woman and, more hiddenly, the child.

It has often occurred to me that two towering masters of psychology are curiously supportive of the dynamic of the Blessed Trinity hazarded in these pages. I suppose that one of the most power-ful themes introduced by Jung is his theory of archetypes – those deep down patterns stamped on the human psyche that seem to programme many of our responses to life and operate in the indi-vidual or the collective unconscious. Ultimately, perhaps, archetypes stem from the one basic pat-tern of our image of and likeness to the Trinity itself. It is a pattern of that mutual giving and receiving which seems to pervade human activity and emerges as an ingrained instinct for communi-cation. Even Jung's attractive theory of the *anima* and *animus*, united and present in man or woman, suggests that our gender difference is but a created image of the relationship between the Father and Word bonded in the Spirit of Love. Each of us is an individual person but we are stamped with a triune bias that would make one of the many.

Something of the same thought seems to emerge from the popular impression that Freud's theories, at least in the domain of psychotherapy, reduce ultimately to the area of sexuality. This may be a crude presentation of a great man's thought but it does contain a powerful though limited truth. In our stammering language the inner life of the Trinity is described as the total gift of one Person to another in love, a union of Persons in one. If we are made in this image and likeness then personal communication on many levels is going to be a characteristic of human behaviour. It will surface in every aspect of life from language, customs and taboos and all that forms us into groups. Such personal and mutual communication in self-gift does have a most powerful expression in rightly ordered sexuality where the relationship is precisely one of person given to person in mutual love. In fact, it has been said of marriage and in all reverence could be said of the Blessed Trinity, that this is 'the nearest and dearest of all relationships'. Freud's intuition does contain a profound but limited truth reflecting the relationships of its triune exemplar but it seems to restrict basic human behaviour to the area of sexuality. This, of course, is by no means the only or most fundamental activity of the spiritual and rational beings that we are.

A final word. Why then, if sexuality is of such dignity, is it so hedged about by Christian sacrament or even pagan taboo? Curiously enough the answer seems to lie in the very splendour of all created things. It is a splendour caught from and imaging the very splendour of God and immortalised by Hopkins, "Creation is charged with the grandeur of God; it will shine out like shining from shook foil". There is a hidden radiance and attraction about created things and where resemblance is closest to divinity there the attraction becomes most fascinating and even dangerously overpowering. Sexuality in the right context does carry with it the mutual and fruitful ecstasy of persons given and united in one but where we have become grabbers rather than givers the temptation is to steal for self-satisfaction and the gift can turn sour. It becomes, as Shakespeare puts it, "An expense of spirit in a waste of shame". You get a glimpse of such dangerous fascination in the story of Lucifer who seems to have been created closer to the likeness and splendour of God than any other of the angels. Instead of revering the gift he came to see himself as equal to God and in that moment fell. Echoes of his ambition linger in temptation of Adam and Eve, "You shall be as Gods". And ever afterwards the great image of God, mirrored in us as masculine and feminine, tends to drag our gaze from the Giver of this splendid gift down to the deadly realms of self-satisfaction and domination. And yet, despite the degradation of our gutter press, sexuality is basically a radiant symbol of our mysterious triune origins where equality and complementarity reign for ever. In the face of modern feminism it seems that male chauvinism is on the decline and maybe there is a change of heart leading at last to the mutual appreciation planned for us in Paradise.

9

The Giving of Gifts

In one way or another St John thumps out his basic contention that "God is love", and the characteristic of love is, of course, giving. We give presents at Christmas; we give parties for friends and lovers give rings or exchange *billets doux*. It would be hard to imagine any affectionate situation without an exchange of gifts which, in the case of martyrs or heroes, is the supreme gift of life itself. Captain Oates, of the ill-fated South Pole Expedition, "walked willingly to his death in a blizzard to try and save his comrades beset by hardships."

"God is love" and we, the human image and likeness of God, reveal our origins by these exchanges of gifts for he is 'Goodness pouring Itself out' in a torrent of personal Self-giving. Instinctively we are moved to imitate this inner dynamic of the Trinity. Now oddly enough this giving so characteristic of love always seems to be costing. It is true that love does not count the cost and parents do not begrudge hours spent at the bedside of a sick child but giving does cost and this mysterious element of sacrifice seems to hover over every aspect of human generosity. Even in our relations with the world of spirits costing sacrifice surfaces as a central mystery and you find the sacrifice of human victims in civilisations as far apart as the Aztecs of South America and the druids associated with Stonehenge. Behind their rituals, sometimes majestic and sometimes horrific, there lies the fundamental desire to give gifts to the gods in the hope of gaining their love and friendship. The blueprint of gift-giving is stamped on creation even though, here on earth, this impulse to give is always costing.

And yet our western civilisation seems to have blurred the very notion of sacrifice and all that goes with it – priest, victim and a divine being. Just think of the things made trivial in headlines "MP 'sacrifices' job to marry secretary"; or "'victim' wife of faithless husband". And as we go on to read about grim human sacrifices among primitive tribes we wonder what on earth is happening. Definitely not something for this scientific age. Yet, just why is history shot through with sacrifice in a thousand different forms or why this compulsion to sacrifice even in the face of hi-tech cynicism? Above all, what is happening in the sacrifice of the Mass? This brings me to an attempt to recapture something of the meaning of this elusive concept of sacrifice. I would like get back to basics and make a huge detour which wanders through the dynamics of a budding romance between boy and girlfriend.

It revolves around that ingredient so essential to such a situation – a box of chocolates.

For years I have felt that such a box answers many of life's problems – birthday presents, ruffled feelings or the awkward moments of a strained love affair. There is mystery caught up with such a gift and part of it is the sense of personal worth it conveys. I knew a nun who first looked at the stamp on her letters; "Am I a first or second class person?" Somehow personal worth had crept into the situation. She knew that the value of the gift is a coded message of esteem for a friend. So too, chocolates are speaking and Black Magic is more eloquent than Mars Bars. "You are a Black Magic person for me and this box is some small token of it. It cost me the earth but what of that if it can deepen our love?" Friendship does not count the cost and, in the last resort, will give not chocs but life itself. "And for Bonnie Annie Laurie I would lay me doun and dee." Somehow this box of chocolates leads us into the mysterious realm of costing sacrifice.

Basically then, sacrifice seems to be concerned with making friends, covenants or alliances and the gifts we offer are so sensitively charged precisely because they represent me, myself. If you refuse the box I feel hurt because in refusing my gift you have rejected me. If you open it with delight then my spirits soar. What of a week's wages if heaven smiles and the two of us munch away happily together. I, the giver, was in the gift and acceptance assured me of your friendship.

But there is more to it than that. Before these non-smoking days, an offer of a cigarette was no more than a polite gesture but chocolates hint at life and death because they are food and food is life. An offer of Black Magic is an invitation to share in my life, my most precious possession. In your acceptance we share life itself and that is the closest bond of friendship. Both giver and receiver are enriched in a profound communion feast and sacrifice has realised the lover's dream of coming closer to his beloved.

It begins to dawn on us why chocolates can deal so effectively with most of life's problems, so many of which are tangled up with strained or broken friendships. This box has foreshadowed the basic elements of sacrifice – gift, giving and acceptance – all with the hope of making or healing living relationships. You can sense the growing friendliness as each sweet melts in the mouth. And this brings to mind yet another element in this business of sacrifice – the meaning of the word 'victim'. In its role of forging friendship the chocolate seems to be getting lost and losing its very identity. And this precisely is what happens to any victim-gift as it achieves its tasks of go-between. It is "laying down its life for its friends." The gift has become a victim and I have always felt deeply for the fatted calf which died amidst merrymaking to seal the reunion of a father with his prodigal son. Victims, even in the shape of chocolates, really do solve many of life's problems but the cost to themselves seems, at first, total.

It is now high time to look at sacrifice itself which is so ingrained in human cultures down the ages as they try to befriend their gods. The pages of Scripture are full of abhorrence for such terrible rites as those of the god Moloch in which innocent children were thrown alive into a furnace, shaped in the likeness of the god. Or again, the king Agag sacrificed his only son in the hope of staving off Israel's assault on his city. Those who have lived near primitive societies will know that rumours of present day human sacrifices still persist and that the Bible accounts of them are not so out of date after all. Sacrifice, secular or profane, is a constant in our history.

We recoil from such memories but there is a kind of logic about these horrific deeds. In trying to make friends with their gods men were giving their most precious possessions as gift-offerings. Your victim, whether chocolate, lamb or human being, always represents you the giver, the suppliant offering your precious self in the hope of being accepted. The more costly the victim-gift, the greater the token of the god's worth in my eyes. Carry this logic to its conclusion and what more costly than a human being endowed with life, that most precious of all gifts, a life that represents my own? The gesture of offering is sealed by the destruction of the victim as proof positive of the total nature of the gift, nothing is being held back. It is an act of absolute trust in the god's benevolence to make a noble response and we think of Abraham willing to offer his son Isaac in just such a context. In the last resort the greatest love will lay down its own human life and not that of a substitute victim. It dies for love of its friends. The hunter in the old song protests to Vilna, the witch of the wood, "Would I not die for you, dear, if I could?"

It would be wrong to think that sacrifice is a one way affair, a *cri de coeur* to unresponsive gods, It is always seeking a return of friendship which is another way of saying that it is seeking divine communion. If your gift, your victim has been accepted by the other girlfriend or goddess – then it becomes special because it has been taken into their divine life and so becomes transfigured. A box refused is a sorry thing but if it is accepted, opened and shared then it becomes 'heavenly'; now we really are in communion with one another. She is now offering back her life to you in this transfigured gift and you are literally eating the food of the goddess. Your lives have reached the goal of union in immortal friendship. Only one response is appropriate – mutual esteem and thanksgiving. As St Augustine remarked, "Lovers sing each others' praises".

So far we have been seeing sacrifice in terms of human friendship but its basic meaning is 'making holy'. If you remember the penny catechism you will recall that sacrifice is the offering of a victim, by a priest, to God alone in token of his sovereign dominion. Which is to say that sacred sacrifice is all about adoration of and communion with God. Does this clash with our notion of human love and the making of friends which we have stressed with our box of Black Magic? I do not think so because love songs and poetry use the language of adoration with great ease, knowing that worship, in the long run, is love burning at its brightest. 'Divine, adorable, worshipful' come naturally to lovers who, as image and likeness, are hinting at the meaning of sacrifice which is precisely loving worship of God. Even at our most earthly, we are still copycat images of the Triune God where personal self-gift is the eternal law of love. Ultimately sacrifice becomes the folly of the cross as Christ lays down his life for God and friends. "Into your hands I commend my spirit", and to this offering the Father replies with resurrection life in the gift of the Holy Spirit. It is true that we feel a repugnance to the very idea of sacrifice and especially towards ritual sacrifice. It is perhaps a healthy response since the basic meaning of 'sacrifice' is 'make holy' but in a rather unholy world this is going to lead to ugly confrontations – trying to go straight amidst a gang of crooks is bound to be difficult. Our revulsion to this association of repugnance with painful sacrifice springs, not only from the pain of such confrontations but also from a sense that in a friendly, not hostile, environment there is a mysterious gladness about the most costing of givings. This lift of the heart witnesses to the real meaning of 'making holy' in a redeemed world. You simply could not stop a Mother Teresa from a costing but glad generosity.

At this point it might help to summarise this

rather breathless analysis of sacrifice. The notion of it has become blurred in our hi-tech civilisation and to recapture something of its nature chocolates had something to say since chocs and sacrifice are both concerned with friends in a small communion love feast. The box represented the giver and its costliness gave some idea of the worth of the beloved. If accepted, the gift becomes one with the other and if given back it unites the giver with the beloved's 'heavenly' life. This sharing of life is the deepest form of friendship. As for the chocolate, it became a victim, lost to the giver but becoming enhanced by the other's acceptance. It seemed to get swallowed up and lose its identity in the communion banquet but it lives on, personified, in the mutual love evident in the lover and beloved. Chocs leave both in a mood of praise and thanksgiving and the whole little drama hints at the supreme sacrifice made by God's Only Son. As the human and divine image of God's goodness, he does on earth what he, the Person of the Word, has been doing eternally in heaven – giving himself totally to the Father in the Spirit of Love and receiving life back, enhanced, at the resurrection. We too offer ourselves with Christ in the sacrifice of the Mass and the Father responds with the return gift of his Victim-Son in his risen glory. Jesus then breathes upon us the Spirit of Love to give us the supreme gift of divine life. The cross cost the victim's life but true love, such as this, gladly counts the cost.

Reader: When dealing with something so sacred

as Christian sacrifice, the chocolate box image comes across as trivial. Could you not substitute a more noble gift like bread, meal or even a wedding ring?

Author: A chorus of friends has said as much. My difficulty is to bring out the true nature of sacrifice, not as a costing and brutal gesture, but as a joyful communion in friendship through a life-giving gift, come what may.

This means seeing sacrifice in some kind of loving ambience for only friends or lovers disregard its cost. Bread, meal or ring do not evoke this ambience so completely as the universally loved situation of a romance. Here the joyful aspect of costly sacrifice is paramount. Diamonds might have done but in them is no sharing in a life exchanging communion meal.

Reader – Hm!

10

The Perfect Response

The gospels reveal to us that life in the Blessed
Trinity is a glorious circulation of personal self-
giving. "All I have is yours, Father, and all you
have is mine" and the driving force of all this, as
Christ himself insists, is love. He has come "that
the world may know that I love the Father" and this
twice evokes the awesome response, "This is my
beloved Son." This mutual exchange of love
between Father and Son was revealed as the Holy
Spirit when the Dove descended upon Jesus, newly
baptised, in the Jordan. It is a pattern of self-giving
that underlies the whole of creation as it mirrors the
eternal self-giving of God, who is 'Goodness ever
overflowing'. It is something half guessed at in the
endless cascade of a waterfall or in the ebb and
flow of the tides. It comes to a climax of love in the
Son's birth, death and resurrection as the Father
gives us the Incarnate Word and as the Son offers
himself back to the Father, taking us with him as
his redeemed brothers and sisters.

This is why any manifestation of 'overflowing goodness' deeply stirs us who are made in God's image and likeness much in the same way that caged birds flutter their wings at the flight of wild geese high overhead. If God, our exemplar is – to put it crudely – a kind of "Giving Machine" – then we copycat creatures will feel a glad response at any experience of giving, at any act of generosity. The dying Philip Sydney is immortalised for directing the cup of cold water to a desperately wounded soldier whose "need is greater than mine". Fr Kolbe volunteered and took the place of a prisoner condemned to starvation death in a concentration camp. In such cases, and even in the small unremembered kindnesses of life we, the image, are somehow gladdened for we are in fact resonating with the glorious harmony of self-giving love in our exemplar, the Trinity. Such responses were to achieve perfection in the heart of Christ who, in face of deadly opposition, was determined to give love for love. He came to do what we were created for and yet failed to do – "always to please the Father". God, like any father, longs for children to come and delight his heart.

Echoes of this infinite yearning reverberate in famous texts where before the foundation of the world, "He destined us to be his sons through Jesus Christ…", since "his delight was to be with the children of men." It almost seems as if creation were called into being simply because 'Overflowing Goodness' could no longer restrain itself from an outward expression of its inner Trinitarian life.

The plan for all this is being revealed in the opening pages of the Bible as they set an elaborate stage for the entrance of us human beings, made in his image and likeness. The plan was taking shape in this fair cosmos created out of nothing and scientists are now suggesting that the first few milliseconds of the 'big bang' were programmed towards organic and human life. Nothing was left to chance.

A canny old theologian, Duns Scotus, no less, held the fascinating theory that creation would not be a perfect expression of the inner life of the Trinity unless God personally entered into it to return infinite love to himself from within it. This was why the Father would send Christ as its crowning king even though sin, in some mysterious manner, should confuse the issue. Sin might mean the Son's coming as a suffering redeemer but through the resurrection he would yet reign in the role of king giving back to the Father adoring and loving children. Despite the cost in suffering, the Father's plan could not be frustrated by our hostility. Jesus would offer from the heart of creation the perfect love longed for by his Father. For all the shame and rejection of Calvary, sin would yet serve.

Even so the Lord would come, not as an intruder, but as a guest. St Bernard pictures the whole of creation begging Our Lady to hesitate no longer in making the invitation; to take the awesome step of uniting creator and creature by her. "Yes; be it done to me according to thy word." She did so and the Word did become flesh, uniting God with the very same dust of this earth as ourselves and here we had at last the perfect response. The Father is loved and adored perfectly from within this cosmos for the God-man returns to his Father the gift of himself with the same love that he, the Word, had given to the Father in the Trinity from all eternity. But he now returns as a victim and when Mary and Joseph presented the child in the temple they were prefiguring Christ's sacrificial response as they offered him back to the Father. Their ritual offering would become definitive on the cross – a spear through his victim-heart and, through hers, Simeon's sword.

Had there been no hostility to Christ's coming, no accusing Jewry, no mocking Roman soldiers, no rebelliousness in us then Christ maybe would have reigned gloriously as Shepherd King with the Chosen Race as his court. His people, the Jews, would then have become ambassadors of the good news to the rest of the world. But, in those cryptic words, "by the devil's envy sin entered the world", paradise was lost and the whole desolate story of deceit, violence and death began the long history that still spatters the pages of our newspapers. In very simplistic terms, you can see in Christ's life the whole 'chocolate box saga' for he was, so to speak, that victim chocolate, swallowed up in death, uniting God the Tremendous Lover with redeemed and beloved mankind. "My son was dead," said the prodigal father, "but has come back to life", and the new life offered is precisely the Holy Spirit. Victim chocolates, being food, were a sharing in life and the victim Christ, returning from heaven at the resurrection, breathed new divine life on the apostles saying, "receive the Holy, life-giving Spirit".

Now this would be far off and long ago were it not for the Mass which daily climbs all the steps of sacrifice. And this is not just a kind of stage performance to keep the Christ-event fresh in mind. It is more like a super-video that could actually bring events live before us. If you closed your eyes at Mass and St John closed his on Calvary, you would both be present to the same event where a sacrificial gift is being offered in the hope that its acceptance will bring a share in the life of the beloved. In the Mass, Jesus is this victim-gift offering himself as one of us to the Father and our sure hope is that in Holy Communion the glorified victim will return to breathe on us the life-giving Spirit. It happened to the apostles after his resurrection and at Mass it happens to us.

If a box of chocolates, the simple victim-gift between lovers, can lift them into the seventh heaven as she shares this sweet food with him... what of the graced banquet of the Mass? Here priest-giver and victim-given are one and the same, wholly intent on making us sharers in divine life, to make us, as the eastern church insists, 'divinized'. Thankful praise is the only response and it is no wonder that the Mass is called 'Eucharist', *the* thanksgiving, for it is bringing about the Father's original plan for our world. This was to have been a created and family expression of the inner life of the Trinity from which his divine Son would offer as King the adoration and love of all creatures and through sacrifice Jesus has now made this possible. The Eucharist gives into our hands this perfect response of creator to his Father. Although the real presence and sacrifice of Jesus are probably uppermost in our belief during the Eucharist there is the further thought that he was also trying to make clear to the apostles, by a parabolic gesture, the meaning of the morrow's crucifixion. Just as food is life-giving and lost to itself when eaten, so on the cross Christ will give his life to them and the Church at total cost to himself. This is hiddenly revealed in his gesture of breaking the bread and giving the wine to be consumed by them. Food of his sacramental body and blood lost to itself at the supper would give them life, just as his death on the cross would offer them eternal life at the resurrection.

At Mass, we the images and likeness, can at last be what we were intended to be – beloved children of God living with the very life of God. We can now adore the Father in Spirit and in Truth, sharing in Christ's perfect response. It really boils down to this business of giving, so evident in the gift of Person to Person in the Trinity. From experience we know giving is the costing jewel of human living. We shy off from the selfish man whilst generosity always compels our admiration. History has never forgotten St Martin who slashed in half his soldier's cloak to clothe a shivering beggar nor St Francis who rushed to embrace a leper. Personal unselfishness has a great triune pedigree which sparkles in this business of giving. Nonetheless, like walking on a twisted ankle, generosity does cost. It hurts to unclench our fist and give and that is why Christ called it service with all the sense of effort that the word evokes.

Calvary was his supreme self-gift but it was the climax of a lifetime's giving for he came not to be served but to give costing service. When he spoke the truth it provoked fellow villagers to attempted murder on the brink of the brow of the hill. When a woman in the crowd touched his robe he healed her sickness but the power went out from him draining his strength. He cast out evil spirits but it earned him the reputation of casting out devils by the power of the devil himself. A lifetime of giving cost him dearly as it costs us because the perfect response of self-gift goes contrary to a world mysteriously grown selfish.

Yet generosity is the Trinitarian blueprint for us who are made in the image and likeness and really there could hardly be any other response to one who is 'goodness ever overflowing'. Christ managed supremely to respond to this basic instinct but when it comes to the crunch, we 'fable and miss'. Generosity seems to hover just beyond our reach. Maybe this is precisely because sacrifice always seems to carry with it overtones of suffering so that the basic and glad meaning of 'making holy' gets overlaid with painful associations. Instinctively we cringe where asked to sacrifice our time, money or efforts. Even when the sacrifice is willingly made a costing element is usually implied. "It was great to get our child healed." Nothing was said about having to sell up the house to pay the bills. And the

Scriptures record that Jesus rejoiced to redeem us but nonetheless it led through agony to the cross.

All of which makes you wonder just why the idea of sacrifice, of making holy, should carry these sombre overtones. Does there always have to be a doomed victim? Did the fatted calf have to die to make merrymaking possible; could it not have been led in, garlanded and fêted, to join the fun? If we could imagine an ideal world where selfishness and sin did not abound it might give us a glimpse of sacrifice as enjoyable as any other human activity. The pleasure we have in giving a costly present to a close friend hints at the possibility of a sacrifice free from sadness. This once again brings to mind the eternal happiness of Trinitarian life where each of the Persons is a source of infinite self-giving in love and no shadow of sorrow falls upon such bliss. Total generosity is matched by the return of a like generosity.

This divine giving collides with suffering only when the Person of the Word comes to dwell among hostile sinners. Our instinct to grab rather than give cannot stand the reproach of such overflowing goodness. Like innocent Socrates poisoned by envious townsmen, Christ is drawn inevitably to the cross. But in an ideal world to come, a world saved from selfishness, then at last sacrifice as joyful 'making holy' could be a reality and giving become bliss. In such a Utopia we can see that the victim-gift would not be destroyed or made to suffer in a desperate attempt to atone for offences or to prove unselfishness in the giver. The victim would become pure gift, all tears wiped away and no need for death or destruction.

This harks back to the true significance of the child in the family triad that evokes the divine exemplar. It is the personal manifestation of two person's total gift each to the other and is a victim-gift without sorrow – the life and light of their lives. The child humbly recalls the eternal go-between Gift of the Spirit flowing between Father and the Word. Such is the high dignity of the child as primordial and unharmed 'victim' in the ungrasping world that is yet to come. Ultimately, sorrow yields to joy.

11

Generosity

The quality of overflowing life in the Trinity could be described as 'generosity' and the crucifix reveals both the wealth and the cost of it when lived out in a world that tends to puts 'me' first. It hurts to give for we have become inveterate grabbers and a huge greed lurks in the human heart. You see it writ large in the Swiss bank accounts of political dictators bringing economic ruin on their people or in the food mountains of Europe. No wonder we shy away from the shining example of Christ's generosity and a kind of gloom sets in as we try yet again to give and forgive as he did. Matters are often made worse by a false notion of 'imitating' Christ as we fail to imitate, under our own steam, this self-giving love. The truth is that his kind of generosity is possible only if we are empowered by the "Spirit of Jesus" and only then can we become capable of living and loving as he did. It took Pentecost to lift dispirited apostles into orbit and it takes Baptism to do the same for us. But much of our thought pattern has been moulded and perhaps deflected by a certain kind of spirituality.

The *Imitation of Christ* is a little classic that has powerfully influenced Catholic thought for centuries with its earthy common sense and its uncompromising insistence on the 'imitation' of Christ. It clearly but dauntingly signposts the narrow path to perfection. "How often shall I resign myself?" "Always, yes at every hour as well in small things as in great. I except nothing, but do desire that you be found stripped of all things." Like carrots dangling before the donkey's nose its high ideals often seem to float just beyond our reach. We can become depressed and, as donkeys do, flop down and stop.

The plain truth is that no one can simply decide to imitate Christ's generosity. Most of us cannot even square up to the heroic life of a Mother Teresa of Calcutta, much less to the imitation of Christ and left to ourselves we are powerless. He is the God-man carrying out a task impossible to us. He lived sinless, offered the perfect victim on the cross for our redemption, rose from the dead and then breathed on us the new life of the Holy Spirit. He did not come to give us a correct pattern of living, a kind of living-rule for us to imitate and then disappear. He came to empower us by baptising us into the new life of the children of God. We have all seen compressed air drills breaking up concrete roads with the greatest of ease as pneumatic power takes over from pick and shovel. Now, curiously enough, the Greek word for 'Spirit' is 'Pneuma'.

Christian living and giving need the pneumatic power of the Spirit to do the 'impossible' job of imitating Christ. With such power we can heave a sigh of relief since it makes generosity and sacrifice possible and takes the sag out of our efforts. St Paul insists that we now serve "in the new life of the Spirit" and that enabled him to give as Jesus gave and so become an authentic image and likeness of Trinitarian generosity ever overflowing.

In a sense Jesus came for one purpose only – to bestow on us this life-giving Spirit. As parents bestow life on the child and so give it all the potentiality to live as they themselves do, so Christ sends from his Father the Spirit who makes us children of God. After the resurrection his first act is to breathe on the apostles, saying "Receive the Holy Spirit..." and at Pentecost the mighty wind, the rocking house and the flames of fire proclaim that the gift has indeed been bestowed. Runaway apostles are now fearless in facing hostile rulers; divine power pours out of them and even their sworn enemies admit that extraordinary miracles are being wrought. The apostles are no longer trying desperately to imitate Christ. They are now children of God living from the new root-gift of the Spirit which enables them to be 'other Christs' and bear much fruit even as he did . Without Christ's Spirit we are a like a powerful car – it may have great potentiality to zoom from zero to ninety in seconds but without petrol, motor spirit, it is static. The saying is true that Christ has no other eyes, no other hands than ours to do his work but we are helpless without this divine energy of the Spirit. It also has been said that at the resurrection we were plugged into God but at Pentecost, the power was switched on.

If generosity is the hallmark of Christianity then it should be most clearly seen where the image and likeness of the Triune God is most manifest. And that brings us back to our starting point – the family of many persons in the unity and love of home. Family generosity is not only pleasing to contemplate but, as Chesterton indicates, is also very efficient simply because it is coming close to being what it was intended to be – the created expression of the inner love and life of the Trinity. Being fortunate enough to come from a family of seven children, I now wonder at the cheerful way my parents brought us all up on shoestring wages; how day after day three meals turned up from an old coal-burning kitchen range; how all seven were nursed at home through measles, mumps and chickenpox and how all packed up and went for a two weeks holiday on one small boat. Other families would mingle with ours and build up lifelong friendships.

The planning and logistics of such expeditions would have graced the War Office – it was so cost-effective. It just had to be since humanly speaking seven children into one small wage packet won't go. All this happy generosity of parental self-giving was sustained by prayer and the hidden power of the Holy Spirit.

As if to authenticate this family expression of the Trinitarian life all the indications of the Spirit's activity seemed present. His wisdom, counsel and understanding radiated from my parents even though, like all mothers and fathers, they had no previous experience of raising a family. Hidden strength, another of the Spirit's gifts kept them going in stormy times. The penny catechism had impressed on us children that these were the gifts of the Spirit which should blossom in the fruits of the Spirit and sure enough these continually cropped up. Love, joy and peace were patiently, even sternly, fostered among the personality clashes inevitable among a family that seated nine or more at table. Among long-suffering elders gentleness, kindliness and goodness mysteriously survived. More hidden-ly, though undeniably present, were those spiritual charisms which are given to individuals for the common good of the community. Among them was the faith that could move mountains of anxiety during sickness or financial crisis and there were small miracles of healing in bodies and relation-ships. Even the Cinderella of charisms, the discern-ment of spiritual evil threatening family unity, showed up as a kind of sixth sense kept sharp by the prayer life of my mother and father.

This small family image of the Blessed Trinity was a demonstration and realisation of the Father's life-giving power; of Julian's 'Mother Christ' nurs-ing us all to maturity and of the Spirit's loving strength that enabled us to live in Christian generos-ity. Many persons living the oneness of home is the family's grass root testimony to the Trinitarian God who is, so to speak, 'Generosity, ever overflowing'.